AN APPEAL TO THE PATRIOT

An Appeal
to the
Patriot

❧

WILLIAM C. BROWNLEE

Righteousness exalteth a nation; but sin is a reproach to any people.
—Proverbs 14:34.

CURIOSMITH
MINNEAPOLIS

Published by Curiosmith.
Minneapolis, Minnesota.
Internet: curiosmith.com.

Previously published by THE AMERICAN TRACT SOCIETY, 1831.

The "Guide to the Contents" was added to this edition by the publisher.

ISBN 9781946145239

GUIDE TO THE CONTENTS

GUIDE TO THE CONTENTS *(Continued)*

An Appeal to the Patriot

BY WILLIAM C. BROWNLEE, D. D.

Righteousness exalteth a nation; but sin is a reproach to any people.—PROVERBS 14:34.

Without a government, no nation can maintain its place or existence among the other nations of the earth. Against violence without, and anarchy within, its struggles for existence would be feeble and short.

A government, in order to promote a nation's happiness and prosperity, must be a *free* government. With the fall of its liberty, and its free institutions, public prosperity and happiness will quickly vanish from a nation.

Hence, whatever tends, in any way, to produce anarchy, or even to mar a nation's liberties, or to weaken the energy of her magistracy, is a curse to a nation; and, on the contrary, whatever has a tendency to consolidate the government, and to shed a freshness of life and vigor over her free institutions, is to be classed among a nation's greatest blessings.

There is another class of principles which must also be noticed here. Civil government is the ordinance of God. This is manifest from reason and the Holy Scriptures: "The powers which be, are ordained of God."[1] This implies, that it is his will that there should be a government among men. This is as certainly true, as that he has willed the existence and the happiness of men and of nations.

No specific form of government has, indeed, been prescribed on the pages of his Holy Word. To do that work was no part of the office of divine revelation. That has been left to man by God, to be discovered and adjusted by the powers of reason and judgment which he has bestowed upon him. And there is a plain rule and guide in this matter, presented to the wisdom of individuals and nations. Since God wills the existence and happiness of nations—and since he can never cease to do this, as long as his divine goodness and benevolence are exercised towards his creatures, and as long as he chooses to preserve their existence in a natural capacity—of consequence, that form of government is the most consonant to his will, which does promote, in the highest degree, a nation's prosperity and happiness.

Hence, we know how to estimate all kinds of government which are administered by force; such

1 Romans 13:1.

as those of the Old World, where the tyrant reigns in darkness, surrounded by his armed slaves; and where the influence of his power quenches the light of knowledge, banishes religion and sound morals, and covers the land with darkness and the shadow of death. There, military bands patrol the streets and guard the highways; there, the property and the lives of the subjects are placed at the disposal of the capricious and cruel tyrant; there, is no room for the exercise of moral principle between the ruler and his subjects; there, the virtues wither and die; there, the inhabitants are "tenants of the grave—the animating principle is gone; they are merely moving masses of flesh and bones."

Such governments have been permitted by God to exist upon the earth, in order to be the scourges of guilty nations. They exhibit, in an impressive manner, the necessary consequences of vice and irreligion upon a nation. As certainly as these become general and national, so certainly do they bring down upon a government and a people utter and irremediable ruin. And, in view of this, how anxiously should every patriot, and every Christian, lend all his aid, and all his influence, to prevent and correct those evils which will bring down on ourselves the same degradation and ruin!

Our republican form of government is, by the favor of Heaven, the perfect contrast of what has been noticed. It is a *government of persuasion*.

The constitutional rights and duties of the magistracy are distinctly marked out, and the extent of their powers clearly defined. They are the servants of the public; and the conditions of their service are, that they promote the interests and the happiness of the nation. In return, the people honor, love, and sustain them. They are mutual blessings to each other.

Under the former classes of government, it is evident, an intelligent and active population cannot exist; neither is there place for pure religion and sound morals. These cannot exist, to any considerable extent, where tyranny reigns; and tyranny cannot breathe, nor exist, where intelligence, morality, and true religion bear sway. And hence, we arrive at this important maxim: *By an intelligent and moral people only, can a pure republic, and free institutions, be sustained and perpetuated.* Of consequence, when the public opinion is the voice and will of the sovereign—that is, the people—nothing can be more important than the illumination of the public mind, and the cultivation of the morals of the people. This is essential to a government of persuasion: it would speedily sink without this. Just in proportion as the mass of the people are enlightened, virtuous, and moral, will that government stand strong, and that country flourish and be happy; and just in proportion as the channels of knowledge are blocked up, or its salutary streams poisoned by error and atheism, will the public mind be corrupted and depraved; vice and immorality will flow over the land, weakening the hands of the magistracy, bidding defiance to the laws, and sweeping all into the vortex of misrule, anarchy, and destruction.

There are three considerations growing out of the above principles, which claim our notice in this discussion.

1. A free government, and its institutions, can flourish only where intelligence, and the civic and moral virtues, flourish in the community.

2. The civic and moral virtues flourish only where a true Christian principle is cherished, in its life and vigor, among a people.

3. A true Christian principle is produced and cherished only by the means of Heaven's appointment, namely, the Gospel, the ministry, the Holy Sabbath, and its institutions.

And here it is proper to introduce *two* explanatory observations, before we advance any farther in our discussion.

1. We advocate *no union of church and state.* Such a union every honest Christian in these United States most earnestly deprecates and opposes; we honestly believe it to be contrary to the interests and happiness of each of them, equally. It is a fact established by historical evidence, that it has been a heavy curse to the church in the Old World, since

the *delusive* prosperity of the days of Constantine. What we are here advocating is simply this, the necessity of a genuine Christian principle pervading and animating the minds of ruler and people, in order to the promotion of pure virtue and sound morals in the nation. The existence of such a Christian principle in the hearts of our rulers, can no more imply a union of church and state, than the existence of mathematical science in their minds can create a union of mathematics and the state. Nor can the zeal of the magistrates, employing their influence as Christians to promote religion, as the basis of public morals and the safety of the state, ever be construed, even by the purest jealousy, into any such tendency.

2. We do not maintain that sound morals and a Christian principle *are essential to the existence* of a government. The subject of our discussion is, the best means of securing the well-being and perpetuity of our republic and free institutions, existing, as they do, among a Christian people. The Roman republic was a government "ordained of God,"[1] but surely, had there been in that pagan government those redeeming and sustaining elements of which we speak, its institutions had, unquestionably, been more free, its form more vigorous, and, humanly speaking, it had not fallen, as it did, amidst the universal corruption and depravity of its population.

1 Romans 13:1.

I. The necessity of THE PREVALENCE OF INTELLIGENCE AND VIRTUE among the community.

In regard to *the public functionaries*, who occupy so commanding a position in the republic, and whose influence is felt in every circle, it is very obvious that the more virtuous and enlightened they are, the more likely will our free institutions be preserved and perpetuated, and the great end of government attained in the happiness and prosperity of the people.

To a faithful public functionary, the virtues are essential. Without the civic virtues, can he be a faithful *representative*, or a pure patriot, devoted to his country's honor and interests? And can we ever find the civic virtues, and pure patriotic principles, reigning in a mind dark and corrupt, and devoid of sound morals? Never: an effect cannot exist without a cause. Could we make the experiment, and abstract from the assembly of our legislators all sound and liberal views, all patriotic feelings and virtue, and the fear of God, we should just have such another assembly as that in which Robespierre and his associates revelled in vice and atheism, during the Parisian reign of terror.

These virtues are equally necessary in a *legislator*. It is his solemn duty to enact just laws. If the laws, by which both magistrate and people are governed, be unjust, the administration of them cannot be otherwise than a system of iniquity and oppression;

and the land will speedily be covered with the deepest guilt, calling down the vengeance of Heaven. But justice will reign in the land when the legislative assembly have the fear of the Almighty before their eyes, and a virtuous regard to the Most High in all their proceedings.

It is the office of the *executive* to see the laws of the land carried faithfully into execution. He must be fully prepared to defend the rights of his fellow-citizens, as it regards life, liberty, and property; to preserve the purity and fairness of trials by jury, to hear with patience, to discipline his own feelings, to pronounce sentence with impartial strictness, to keep his hand free of bribes, to have no respect of persons in judgment, to mingle justice with mercy, to watch over the public good, to redress grievances with frankness and promptitude, to prevent wrongs, to discourage a litigious spirit, to heal breaches in a neighborhood; in a word, to be a father to the people, and to be pure in character as the ermine of his own robe. But can these virtues, so necessary to qualify the executive, be found in the selfish, immoral, and ignorant man? No, never! Sound morals and religion are the necessary bases of all these civic virtues, which qualify and adorn the magistrate. Take them away, and our judges and advocates would be converted into the M'Kenzies, the Lauderdales, and Jeffries, of infamous memory.

The right of trial by *jury* is one of the brightest

stars in our free institutions, and one of the safest guards of our liberty, lives, and property. With the juror rests a very deep and solemn responsibility: in his safe-keeping, are reposed the honor and the dearest interests of his country and his fellow-citizens. Who could feel himself safe before an ignorant, and vicious, and unprincipled jury? Without intelligence, without morality, without a deep and awful sense of the presence and justice of the Deity, no juryman can do his duty to his country, his fellow-men, and his God. Without these virtues, he will be the mere tool of a corrupt judge: without these virtues, a jury would be converted into a terrific curse to the community. They might sit in judgment, but, like the satellites of Robespierre, they would sit to shield the guilty, to drive the patriot into exile, to plunder the unprotected of their property, and doom the innocent to death.

And the *defenders* of our country, the gallant men of the army and navy, what would they be, without virtuous principles, and a deportment regulated by sound morals? They would speedily be converted into a band of licensed assassins, the oppressors of their country, and the sanguinary instruments of a military despotism. Their prototype we should behold in the Turkish soldier, and the palace guards of eastern tyrants.

A free press, in the hands of wise, virtuous, and patriotic men, is a blessing of inestimable value.

It is the glory and strength of a free government. It throws increasing light on the public mind; it keeps steadily before the view of the people their national rights; it fans the sacred flame of patriotism; it scourges vice and immorality, and makes them shrink from the view of the community; it holds up to the public eye the conduct of men in office, and keeps them under the restraining awe of public sentiment, and in a rigid adherence to the line of their duties; it sounds the alarm at the first encroachment of ambition and power; it concentrates a nation's energies, in sustaining patriotic men and a virtuous government, and in pulling down oppression and tyranny. Hence, as one of the most efficient aids of the ministry and of the magistracy, a virtuous and enlightened press pours a stream of health and vigor over the patriotism of rulers and the virtues of the people; and hence, it fails not to cherish and perpetuate her free institutions.

The history of the decline and fall of the Roman and the Greek republics, affords us an impressive lesson on this point. They had no instrument to effect this national illumination, and create this moral bond of union and strength in the public mind. The want of the press must be enumerated among the main causes of the decline and final overthrow of those ancient republics, by the encroachments of tyranny.

And the events of the recent revolution in

France, 1830, afford us another valuable illustration on this topic. It was a beautiful and happy contrast to the old revolution. There was, throughout, no treachery, no ebullition of atheism, no massacres, no public robbing and plundering, "no insult to a royalist, nor even to a woman," to use the words of La Fayette. All displayed love of order, respect for property, an enlightened and irrepressible spirit of patriotism, an unconquerable love of liberty in citizen and soldier, who hastened to the deliverance of their country in the day of her trouble. And what was the cause of this astonishing difference in the two revolutions? It was, as we believe, in no small measure, the influence of *the press*, which had, for some fifteen years, been illuminating the public mind, and contributing to raise the standard of moral feeling throughout the nation.

On the other hand, if the freedom of the press be cramped, or if it be converted into licentiousness, it will become a terrible scourge to a nation. Who can calculate the extent of the evils which it may originate? According to the extent of its blessings, so may be the extent of its malignant influence. In the hands of atheists and profligate men, it may overthrow the government, and destroy the religion and morals of a nation. Under the control of tyrants, it may rivet the chains of slavery, or hurry a nation into the vortex of anarchy. For the melancholy proof of this, we have only to lift our eyes to the age of Voltaire and Robespierre. By them, the press had been long and shamefully prostituted in the dissemination of their destructive principles.

It is obvious, therefore, that there are few men in the republic who can exert a greater and more salutary influence over the public manners, and our free institutions, than editors and literary men. And it is equally obvious, that there are very few who have it in their power to accomplish a greater extent of mischief to the dearest interests of man. And hence, it is a matter of the greatest importance, that these men should be actuated by virtuous, patriotic, and truly religious principles.

Now, let us conceive a regular system of means, fully adapted to the end, put into requisition, to diffuse over all these classes of men this requisite knowledge, moral, civil, and religious, together with the pure and exalted virtues arising out of a sincere veneration for the DEITY—what a moral force would thence be added to the hands of government; what integrity and honor in our public elections; what salutary laws would emanate from our legislative halls; what fidelity and vigilance in the execution of them; what a moral dignity and worth would shine forth in all the political, and civil, and military departments; what purity of patriotism; what love of truth and justice in our courts; what sacredness in an oath; what a blending of mercy and judgment in the administration; what studious zeal in elevating the honest and capable only, to public stations; what solidity of character in public and in private life; what a righteous love of order and peace; what good feelings in every neighborhood, and in all ranks throughout the land; what a holy rivalship between magistrate and people, to do the greatest good to their common country! Can any thing be deemed more effectual than this, to cherish and perpetuate our free institutions?

On the contrary, let the system of an opposite spirit be carried into effect over the land; let these means be utterly withheld; let there be no counteracting influence put forth against the emissaries of vice, irreligion, and atheism—we are not left to conjecture what the result would be. Under similar circumstances, by the operation of the corrupt principles of human nature, which is the same in all nations and ages, there would be the dreadful recurrence of the scenes of past times: crimes would increase and multiply over the land, to an unparalleled degree; men would bid defiance to the laws and the magistracy; then would follow the horrible revolutionary scenes which have disgraced nations, and plunged them into all the revolting evils of anarchy and atheism!

But we extend our remarks beyond the public functionaries. It is, if possible, of even greater importance to the well-being and perpetuity of our free institutions, that *the people, as a body*, be enlightened and virtuous.

Were our public functionaries the most enlightened and virtuous men in the land, how long would our government and our free institutions flourish, were the great body of our population sunk in ignorance, vice, and infidelity? The *elective power* is lodged with them. As the sovereign, they elect their representatives, and intrust to them the power of enacting laws: from them proceeds the power of the judiciary and the executive. Now, if the fountain be corrupt, the streams cannot be otherwise than polluted. An ignorant and immoral people become the easy dupes of wicked and designing men; their votes will be bartered away, through partiality or mere party feelings, without reference to the honesty and capability of the candidate. Themselves vicious and unprincipled, they would bestow places of power and trust on men like themselves; and speedily would the fatal streams of disease and death be poured through all the offices of our government, and over all the institutions of the land. Liberty would be converted into licentiousness; the sanctity of our courts profaned; justice expelled from her awful throne; the sacredness of an oath treated with scorn; perjury and subornation of perjury would be prevalent to a revolting degree; the laws would, by degrees, be openly contemned and trampled upon; the faithful magistrate would be hurled from his seat, and sent to the dungeon, or the block. The military force might be opposed to the force of the people; but what could they do against the mass of power opposed to them by an infuriate mob? Anarchy and civil war, with all their horrid train of evils, would rage over the land; some military adventurer would, in the public convulsions, grasp the reins of power; and a military despotism would, in a short period, sway its iron rod over the ruins of our free institutions. For, according to the voice of history, uttering its sage admonitions, a people sunk into this condition can be ruled *only by the iron rod of force.*

This dreadful state of things can be prevented only in one way, and that is, by sustaining the reign of the law, and the just power of the magistracy. And these can be sustained only by an enlightened and virtuous community; for such only can duly appreciate the value of free institutions; such only will revere the laws, and obey them; such only will revere the magistracy of their own choice, and be ready to rally around them, in every extremity, when atheism and crime threaten the peace and good order of the state. Now,

II. WHAT ARE THE BEST MEANS OF ATTAINING this illumination of the public mind, and the diffusion of virtuous principles among the great mass of the people?

These means must be in perfect accordance with the genius of our free institutions, and our holy religion. No force can be resorted to. Physical power can never create the principles of religion and virtue. It was the spirit of persecution, which was born in a dark and barbarous age, and which never had any fellowship with the spirit of Christianity, that gave origin to the cruel practice of employing force; but it dies with the expiring barbarism of the dark ages, and the dissolution of the inquisition.

Neither can these holy principles be called into existence by the lectures of schoolmen, or the writings of moralists, solely. The truth is, these, though valuable in their place, can convey no vital principle into the dark and depraved mind of man. The best of advices and instructions may be administered, but it requires a certain principle within the mind to receive and reduce into practice these advices and instructions. The basis of true virtue and sound morals is a spiritual principle of life in the soul of man. Without this, as we are assured by divine authority, "man is dead in trespasses and sins"; and while this moral or spiritual death enchains the mental powers, no spiritual life can exist, no pure and holy actings can be put forth by the soul. Now, no human means nor human agency can awaken this life, and call it forth into active exertions, and the fruits of holiness. "God only can quicken us, who are dead."[1]

In addition to this testimony of the Holy

1 Ephesians 2:1.

Scriptures, we have the evidence of facts. What influence had the splendid lectures of Socrates and Plato, of Tully and Seneca, on the population of Greece and Rome? What influence have the zeal and eloquence of modern moralists had on the body of their followers? And what is the moral character of the great body of the studious youth at home and abroad, even after they have enjoyed the benefit of the ablest instructions from the moral chair? The truth is, the doctrine of morals is, in these philo- sophical systems, usually separated from the holy principles of the religion of Christ; and whenever this has been done, no one single conversion, no one genuine reformation, has ever been effected. The human system of morality, drawn up by the wise and the learned, *can* never communicate the principle of spiritual life; and from the days of Socrates to our times, it never *has* done it.

It is equally certain that *the civil law* of the land cannot be made the instrument of this national and moral reformation. The language which the civil law holds is this: Every man shall be protected in his rights, so long as he commits no crime reached by its penalties; and every crime shall be punished, in order to prevent, so far as the influence of exam- ple and punishment can prevent, the recurrence of a similar crime. But these laws offer no moral nor religious instruction which can beget the spiritual and moral principle of life in the soul. No human wisdom nor power of man can do this: the Deity alone can bestow the gift, and he alone can dictate the means whereby it is conveyed to us.

There are other considerations which add strength to this. There exist in society certain crimes, against which there is no provision by the law of the land, and which, therefore, the law and the magistracy cannot cure: such as avarice, wasting, prodigality, luxury, disrespect to parents and guardians, partiality in voting at elections, etc.

Now, no people become vicious and abandoned at once: the descent to moral degradation is gradual, and at first slow. There are usually small beginnings; and these crimes now specified may be the beginning and first elements of great crimes. They do lead to great and distressing evils in the community. Prodigality and luxury lead to want, and thence drive men, who are the slaves of their passions, to despair and to violent deeds. Disrespect to parents invariably leads to disobedience to their commands; and thence, by the most natural process, to the contempt of public opinion, and contempt of the magistracy, and a proud defiance to the laws. The transition to the most atrocious crimes is thence a matter of course. And the partiality of a people's vote, in a day of political excitement, has not unfrequently elevated an unprincipled and wicked man to power, who has caused, in his time, unspeakable damage to the morals of the people, and the liberties of his country.

Now, there is not a patriotic magistrate in the land, who will not be anxious to cure and prevent these lesser evils, which necessarily lead to the commission of crimes and great disorders in the community. But it is perfectly obvious, that the true means to effect this do not really belong to his office, *as such*. The civil law has no penalties, and can have no penalties against them: he cannot exert force against them. The truth is, these vices which we have enumerated can be displaced and destroyed only by the introduction of the opposite principles and virtues.

And this is not all: there are certain duties which the law of the land cannot reach, or enjoin on the subject. They are such that they cannot be enforced by a penalty, which is essential to a law—such as gratitude, benevolence, fidelity in friendship, correct education of children, forgiveness of injuries, charity, piety to God.

The neglect of these will, as in every case of moral crime, always issue in some other delinquency; and thence, in time, they wax worse and worse. But the diligent cultivation of them in early life will lead to virtues of a higher order, and to fixed principles of morality among a people.

As certainly, therefore, as the patriot and magistrate does betake himself to the proper and moral means of cherishing these virtues, does he prevent crime; as certainly does he promote a growing vigor of moral principle throughout the community; and thence does he not only promote the happiness and prosperity of the public, but he strengthens and consolidates the free institutions of his country.

Let us rise a step higher. It is a prominent duty of the magistrate, and all our public functionaries, to employ every means which God puts into their power to *prevent crimes*. It is their duty, for instance, to prevent peculation and fraud on the public treasury; but this cannot be done, unless men in public employment be rendered honorable, just, and pure. And such virtues cannot exist, in the solidity of a persevering principle, without strict virtue and the fear of God in the heart. It is their duty, moreover, to prevent smuggling, and similar illicit practices, which bring damage to the public revenue, and serious injury to the fair and honest dealer. And what would be the most effectual method of compassing this end? Vigilance and military force would do something towards it: exemplary punishment might strike a terror into their minds for a season; but unquestionably the radical cure would be the spreading of useful knowledge, and of moral and religious principles, over the minds of that lawless class of men, and over that part of the community in which they are trained up, and also over the minds of those citizens who participate in their unlawful gain. They are bound, moreover, to prevent perjury and the subornation to perjury, even as they are bound to take away every hindrance in the way of impartial justice. And by what means can the patriotic magistrate cure or prevent this revolting and injurious evil in our courts? Can persuasion or force operate on a mind in which there is no virtuous principle, no fear of God, no regard to futurity? No: the only way to accomplish it is, to inspire into the minds of men an abhorrence of profane swearing, which tends always to lessen the solemnity of an official oath; to fill them with a deep and awful veneration of the Deity; and to bring them under the influence of a firm faith of *the judgment to come*, and the assurance of "the perdition of ungodly men."

On the contrary, were we to remove all the existing restraints—were we to take away from the midst of society the strict love of truth—were we to abstract, or even impair, in the public mind, the holy veneration and fear of the Almighty—were infidelity to spread its atheism over our population, unchecked by Christian influence or example—how speedily would perjury, and subornation to perjury paralyze the arm of justice, and deprive us of the judiciary, or turn it into a curse and a national scourge!

The same observations apply to the prevention of other crimes, such as bribery and corruption, the spirit of quarrelling and litigation, forgery and counterfeiting, intemperance, lewdness, stealing, robbery, murder, and, in a word, tumults, insurrections, and high treason. *Out of the depraved heart*, we are told by the highest authority, *do all these crimes proceed:* that is the fountain whence these bitter and deadly streams issue; and every fresh indulgence widens the channel, and adds fury to their raging torrents. Now, no physical power can dry up this fountain: it may cut off some streams, it may throw a temporary barrier in the way, and so check them for a season. It is the Holy Spirit of God only who can enter in and dry up this deep and deadly fountain; he alone can make the living waters of life spring up there in their stead; he alone can make holy and virtuous principles flow forth.

Nothing short of this can effect the object; and just so far as we cherish and extend the influence of these holy principles, awakened into life in us by the power of God, do we obtain an effectual remedy for all those crimes. By the changing of the heart, are its principles of action changed; and thence there is a change of the outward deportment. Make the tree good, and the fruit becomes good; make the fountain pure, and the streams will be pure. Awaken the conscience to a sense of the divine presence; call into active life the love of God and virtue; and you thence convey to the mind a new train of sentiments and feelings; you give a new tone and real elevation to the soul; you make it feel a conscious dignity; the fear and love of God constrain it away from what is vicious and what is mean. You convert a man of bribes into an upright man, the forger and counterfeiter into an industrious citizen, the cheat and peculator into a man of integrity, the liar into a man of veracity, the drunkard into a lover of temperance, the thief and robber into an honest man and a lover of good order. And as this holy and renewing influence pervades the great mass of the people, you convert the boisterous elements of civil tumult, and discord and treason, into benevolence, and patriotism, and all the active charities of life. We arrive at this conclusion, that vices are expelled by the introduction of the opposite virtues; and this holds equally true in regard to the community, as to individuals. And this will guide us to discover, that,

III. The effectual means, under the Spirit of God, to produce and cherish these virtues so necessary to the community, are altogether of A MORAL NATURE.

1. We give a prominent place to *the Christian education of children.* Genuine religion and morality, as we have seen, are connected by the inseparable tie of cause and effect: they cannot exist apart; the presence of the one indicates the existence of the other. A veneration for the Deity, and a pure and living faith in our Redeemer, are the basis of a sound and healthy morality. Now, if *parents* throughout the land, acting the part of Christians and lovers of

their country, were, with the aid of Sabbath-school teachers, diligently to present the divine truths of Christ before the hearts of their children and did they, with earnest and devout instruction, impress on their minds the necessity of pure morals and the fear of God—by the grace of Christ they would early become pious, and grow up in every Christian attainment. And from these family circles would there issue forth throughout our country, a noble race of intelligent, virtuous, and patriotic men, the glory of their country, and her stay and strength in the day of trial. But just as certainly as parents neglect this, and, on the contrary, by their vicious examples, by Sabbath-breaking, by their contempt of the house of God, by their infidelity, add fresh fury to the powers of their young depravity, do they rear up a host of enemies to their country. They light firebrands, and hurl them into the bosom of society!

2. There is another class of men in the midst of us, who are public men, and the most efficient enemies of tyranny and ignorance: we mean *our schoolmasters*. Standing up as the guardians of our youth, and wisely blending civil with moral and religious instructions, they enlighten and train up our future rulers, statesmen, and fellow-citizens; and give them back to their parents and their country, with the pledge of their successful labors conspicuous in their virtues and patriotism. National instruction,

by our common schools and our Sabbath-schools, is natural strength and security, under the blessing of God, the importance of which has never yet been duly calculated. Certainly, it can never be over-rated. It is not *physical* strength we speak of—it is the *moral* strength of an enlightened and virtuous nation of freemen. Let the schoolmaster and the Sabbath-school teacher, then, walk over the breadth and length of the land, and do their duty: the blessings which they bring to the public, in the prosperity and growth of vigor diffused by them over her free institutions, can neither be bought by gold, nor achieved by military prowess.

3. The pious labors of *the minister of religion* are of the greatest importance. He comes forward into the assemblies of his fellow-citizens as God's accredited messenger, charged with the office of expounding his will to men, and sent to beseech them, and woo them over to piety and good works. He brings with his office no worldly pomp, no earthly weapons; he asks the aid of no civil power; he deprecates the union of church and state; he lifts his voice in solemn warnings against it; he comes with unaffected humility and earnestness to teach the ways of God to men; he opposes vice and atheism in all its forms, in high places and low places; he carries in his hand the pure and unadulterated *Gospel of the Lord Jesus Christ*. From that he derives all the weight, influence, and efficacy of his spiritual office.

That Gospel breathes peace and good-will to man; its object is to chase away darkness from the human soul, and thence from the community, by the extensive diffusion of knowledge. It breathes the spirit of liberty in all things civil and religious; it calls on all men to consider this as their unalienable birthright and privilege; it awakens man to a deep sense of his dignity and worth as an immortal being; it brings health and salvation to his soul; it makes him the freedman of the Lord; it enjoins on all the subjects of God's moral government, to "live soberly, righteously, and godly in the world"; it breathes death to tyranny and oppression: in a word, it constrains men to fear God, to honor the magistracy, to love all men.

The Gospel is more than a mere exhibition: it is the instrument, the only instrument, of God's appointment, to beget in us the new life, and all the elementary principles of the purest virtues. Other systems, human in their origin, tell us of the beauty and worth of these; other systems exert a moral influence and persuasion, it is true; but it is the word of the Lord which actually begets in us the new life.[1] It is the only instrument which the Spirit employs for this purpose; and on this principle of life in "the new creature in us," it exerts a progressive influence, cherishing and maturing it, and drawing forth actively each new power into the

1 1 Peter 1:23, 25.

service of God. Hence all these graces of the soul, hence all these virtuous actions in the life, hence all that pure morality in the Christian's intercourse with his fellow-men, which throw a luster over the human character, and render a man a blessing to his family, to society, and to his country.

Now, such being its influence on *individual* character, it is obvious that, wherever its pure and subduing spirit exerts its power over a land, it must chase away darkness from its population, it must banish vice and folly, it must lessen crimes, it must beget an enlightened reverence for the laws, it must make good citizens, it must thence lend a vigor to the arm of justice, and strength to the hands which administer the laws; it must pour the most salutary influence on every portion of our population. It throws its light on the seat of infidelity and atheism, revealing to all who *will* see, their deformity and pestilential evils. It chases from its holy presence the demon of discord, and malignity, and civil broils, and litigation. It turns wars into peace to the ends of the earth: for wherever it is welcomed and embraced in its simplicity and purity, it fills the land with the love of peace, and the love of good order, and harmony, and justice, and righteousness. It breaks no bonds, it dissolves no ties, but those of tyranny and sin. Widely as its influence is felt, does it unite the human family in ties not to be dissolved in time, never to be severed in eternity. The spirit of the Gospel is love, and love is eternal.

4. The *Holy Sabbath*, with the institutions thereof, is inseparable from the Gospel; the one being the *season* of its displays, the other the *means* by which the goodness and grace of God put forth their blessed fruits among us. Its spiritual and moral influence cannot but be of the greatest moment, coming, as it does to the aid of the patriotic parent, the minister, the schoolmaster, and magistrate, in the great moral work of sustaining and perpetuating our free institutions.

If there were no *stated Sabbath*, there could be no stated season for assembling the people; the public instructions, from the preaching of the Gospel, could not be addressed at stated, regular seasons to the great mass of our population. If there had been a day, but no *regular* day, fixed for the Sabbath, the greatest confusion would necessarily have been caused throughout society. And nothing can, for the same reason, be more plain than this, that if God our Sovereign had not fixed that regular and stated season, neither the churches nor the nations of the earth would have been willing, or, indeed, could have been able, to enter into this compact. What had so important a concern in the interest of the whole human family could come, imperatively binding, only from the Father of us all! And it did come from him. For thus saith the Lord, "REMEMBER THE SABBATH-DAY TO KEEP IT HOLY."

There is no device of man, planned and ripened as it might be by ingenuity and wisdom, which can in any way be compared to this divine institution, in the moral and civil influence which it exerts on a nation.

As an institution of *mercy*, it lends its aid to our free institutions. It protects the laboring part of the community, the strong body of the nation, from the oppressions of rich and severe masters. Beyond the reach of their employers' command, each Sabbath-day they rest, and are refreshed.

It brings all classes of citizens into a pleasant social intercourse in its holy convocations; it spreads a delightful cordiality of feeling over all their minds; it unites them, as immortal beings, in one common and great interest; it brings them together under the august presence of Almighty God; it sets before each of them, by its sacred institutions, the affecting tokens of his presence; they meet in a place sacred to his service, before whom the highest angels bow, and the humblest man may worship. The rich and the poor bow together: in equal need, they mingle their prayers at the same throne, and implore, in the same helplessness, the grace of their common Saviour. It has, therefore, a moral tendency to abase the pride of the great. It gives an elevation to the minds of the honest and pious poor; while the rich, the learned, and the great, look around them on their poor, and unlettered, and humble fellow-citizens, they feel a constraint, under the eye of their Maker, to admit in their hearts that these men, whom they despise in the public walks of life, are often more wise and more lovely in the presence of God than themselves. The honest poor rise to the true elevation of their worth; the great are depressed to their proper level. What a salutary influence is here exerted over the community, in favor of our republican government and institutions!

Nor is this all: this institution is "the only means ever devised of communicating instruction to the great mass of the people. Here all may assemble, here all may learn, from the highest to the humblest." And the instruction delivered on this sacred day, is the most important conceivable: it is that by which the noblest of God's creatures, in this province of his empire, are trained up for the noblest and most glorious destinies beyond the grave!

And moreover, while other institutions come with the force of human eloquence and persuasion, still, they are but human, and partial in their results, as general experience has shown. But here, divine wisdom and influence, are put forth in God's institution, by the means and the ministry of his own appointment. And his word of promise, holy and sure, is pledged for the result: "As the rain cometh down, and the snow from heaven, watering the earth, and making it bring forth and bud, that it may give seed to the sower, and bread to the eater; so shall my word be, that goeth out of my mouth: it shall not return to me void; but it shall accomplish that which I please, and it shall prosper *in the thing* whereto I sent it."[1] And the souls and the lives of thousands over all lands where the holy institution exerts its sacred influence, bear witness to the truth, that HE has remembered his promise in faithfulness. And this influence is always visible wherever the Sabbath is. We speak, now, mainly of its *national* blessings. In every place where the Sabbath is kept holy unto the Lord, it invariably begets a peculiar decency of manners, and regularity of habits; it spreads the love of peace and good order in a neighborhood; by the recurrence of the holy season, the deep and awful veneration of the Deity is cherished into an abiding habit; and every civic and moral virtue is nurtured into a vigorous growth, over the whole mass of that population.

A thousand prayers are breathed out on that holy day, from sincere hearts, for their country, for their rulers, for their fellow-citizens, and for all men— that liberty and religion may be spread abroad over the face of the earth; while, at the same time, in the fervor of their devotions, with hearts imbued with the ardent benevolence of the Gospel, deep sympathy is expressed for all those who are suffering under sickness, oppression, wars, and tyranny. Every thing combines, on this season, to fan the

1 Isaiah 55:10, 11.

flame of patriotism, and to strengthen the love of liberty and their devotion to their republican institutions. Thousands over our flourishing republic, as they return, on the sacred day, from their public assemblies, exclaim with patriotic emotion,

> Dear native land! how do the good and wise
> Thy happy clime, thy countless blessings prize!

This moral tendency of the Gospel and its divine institutions, is strongly illustrated by HISTORICAL FACTS AND INCIDENTS.

Let any one open the Holy Bible, and study the moral history of the Jewish nation in the books of Moses, the Judges, the Kings, and the Prophets, and he will perceive, on the one hand, the striking connection between the civic virtues and morals and religion, and on the other the necessary connection between these and the prosperity and happiness of the nation. When the Hebrews neglected the duties of religion, and forsook the Lord God of their fathers, vice and wickedness overflowed the land; every department of the government became corrupt with a corrupt population; the wrath of heaven fell on them, and "they were sold into the hands of their enemies":[1] they were made bondmen and slaves. But when religion and piety flourished throughout all ranks in the land, the prosperous

---

1 Judges 2:14.

and happy government shed the blessings of its wise and mild administration over a free, a virtuous, and happy population; and thus "righteousness exalted the nation."

The same facts are exhibited on the pages of the history of the Eastern nations. We have only to consult the *Universal History,* and particularly the impressive details of *Rollin's History*, and we shall discover the most ample evidence of this. But we may descend to particulars, and come down to later times.

Let any one look into the records of the London Newgate, and listen also to the affecting narratives of the criminals condemned in our own courts, and he will discover that the first step which led these unhappy men into their criminal course, was neglect of parental authority and instruction, contempt of the house of God and religious admonitions and warnings, and Sabbath-breaking. These paved the way for every other crime, and led them to their fatal end!

In what states of our Union are there the fewest crimes? In what districts are found the most intelligent and virtuous citizens? In those, uniformly, where the Holy Sabbath, and the preaching of the Gospel, and all the institutions of Christianity, have been regularly exerting their benign influence on the people from year to year.

In what districts have crimes abounded the

most, such as theft, robbery, lewdness, intemperance, and murder? Just in those parts and among
those classes of the people over whom infidelity and
atheism have been exerting their fatal influences
with untiring assiduity; and where there is no pas-
tor to assemble the people; and where there is no
veneration, nor even respect, for the Holy Sabbath;
and where there is not a church-going people, even
when they might, if they chose, enter the house of
God. In fact, it is obvious to all who have bestowed
the least attention on the subject, that in every family, in every street of our cities, in every district of
our country, where no Sabbath is sanctified, there
is no religion: where there is no Sabbath, there are
no pure morals; where there is no Sabbath, "there
man forgets God, and God gives man up to his own
corrupt ways!" Where there is no Sabbath sanctified, those classes of men who boast of their illumination by philosophy, become sceptics, infidels,
atheists! Where there is no Sabbath sanctified, those
classes of the people who are not enlightened by
philosophy—and they are the great mass of the
population—become degraded by all manner of
vice, and brutalized by idolatry! Every Pagan and
Mohammedan land, every infidel district in town
and country, exhibit the most painful and over-
whelming evidences of these facts.

The history of Missionary enterprises, and the
ecclesiastical condition of nations, throw additional

light on our argument, and strengthen it.

Lift up your eyes, and track the progress of the Gospel and its holy institutions over the different nations of the world. Contrast the Christian districts and villages in the bosom of the nations of ancient Egypt, and Syria, and Greece, and the Roman provinces. What a contrast! It is the contrast of light with darkness, of piety with superstition, of religious homage with shocking idolatry, of purity with revolting abominations, of manly and dignified love of liberty and respect for all the rights of man, with mental degradation and tameness under slavery! Contrast the Christian Britons with the Britons of Caesar's day—the Christian Americans with the red men of the wilderness. What, I pray you, has wrought the difference? The Gospel, and its ministry, and its Holy Sabbath, and its sacred institutions—these have done it. Take these away from the British by the deadly power of infidelity, and the Paganism and Druidism of the Britons would be soon renewed. Banish from our happy republic the Sabbath, and the Gospel, and the ministry; place us under the atheism and power of the infidel mob of our day, or under the dominion of Jesuitism—our happy land would soon lose her liberty and her free institutions, and we should, in a short period, be as the bond slaves of Spain, or Italy, or Austria, or of the dark Pagan lands of Asia!

Contrast, moreover, the moral and political

condition of the twenty-three islands of the Pacific ocean now Christianized, with their condition as described by Cook and other travellers. Withdraw from them the Gospel, the Sabbath, and the ministry; place them under the influence of atheism; the shocking relapse into their former condition would afford us some idea of what this fair republic would in a few years be, if these holy institutions were removed from the midst of us!

In the moral character of Scotland, and her attachment to liberty and her free institutions, and in her glorious struggle in a conflict of twenty-eight years against a ferocious tyranny, civil and spiritual, we perceive in an impressive manner, the influence of popular knowledge, religion, and morals. And the reason is manifest: in no other land, perhaps, has the Gospel of Christ gone forth in such mighty displays of its power; in no other land is the Sabbath more religiously observed. And had it not been for these principles of knowledge, which preserved a clear and mutual understanding among the lovers of freedom, and those moral and religious feelings which nerved their minds, and sent them forward into the field of action in all the ardor of a noble and patriotic enthusiasm, that people had sunk beneath their natural enemy, the Cavalier and the Tory; had it not been for these unsubduable principles, they had lost their civil and religious liberties forever, under the persevering tyranny of the Stuart dynasty.

In the revolutionary struggle of our own country, the great body of the people were a reading and thinking class of men; they possessed enlightened views; and there was a sacred regard to honor, to sound morals, and to our holy religion, throughout the community. And just in proportion to the moral strength of these feelings and principles, was there an unsubduable ardor of patriotism, and devotion to liberty and republican institutions.

But had the mass of our population been as ignorant and vicious as is the degraded population of Mexico and the southern republics in our day, or as the Parisian mob of the old French revolution, they would assuredly have been disgraced by their revolting massacres and blood-thirstiness; and they would have speedily fallen back again beneath their old yoke, or have bowed their necks beneath an infidel directory, or a military despot!

In England, there have been periods when the people displayed a very successful zeal in clinging to their rights and liberties, and in resisting the encroachments of tyrants. And these struggles were always the firmest, most persevering, and successful, in the periods when a mighty impulse had been given to spiritual zeal, piety, and true religion. In the days of her emancipation from the yoke of Popery, it is difficult to say whether her abhorrence of spiritual tyranny, or her love of pure religion and Christian morals, was the most ardent. Contrast this

with her former days, when holy light had not
dawned over her, and the spirit of religion had not
yet awakened her populace, or even her rulers, from
their profound slumbers. When knowledge awakened her, and holy religion inspired her, she rose in
her might, and as easily as the lion shakes the dew-
drops from his mane, did she shake off the chains
and fetters of the tyrant!

In the days of the Commonwealth, when her
patriots maintained the cause of liberty against the
fanatical advocates of the *divine right of unlim-
ited monarchy*, on which side were found the most
enlightened views of the rights of the ruler and
the subject? On which side were found the inex-
tinguishable love of liberty, and the great weight
of solid English character, and morality, and pure
religion? In the camp of the republicans, beyond
a doubt, among the Puritans, where the Sabbath
was held most sacred, and the ministry of Christ
honored, and the pure Gospel preached uniformly
with divine success. And what a contrast did this
present to the camp of Charles I and the court of
Charles II! The Scottish Malignant and the English
Cavalier, the favorites of the Stuarts, united in their
characters the grossest flattery of absolute monarchy and spiritual tyranny, with the most revolting
irreligion, blasphemy. Sabbath-breaking, intemperance, revelling, and an utter contempt of even common decency!

The history of France, also, affords us one of the fullest and most instructive illustrations of our argument. The tyrannical and sanguinary house of Bourbon had inflicted many evils on the Reformed churches and ministry; Charles IX, young in years, but old in crime, struck the first dreadful blow, at the massacre of St. Bartholomew, in A.D. 1572. New tyrants added fresh injuries; and at the distance of about one hundred years from that massacre, in A.D. 1685, Louis XIV revoked the edict of Nantz, and let loose the fiends of persecution. By a succession of cruelties, massacres, and exile, the great body of the faithful ministry of France was destroyed. The rest, a melancholy remnant, pining in obscurity, fell by degrees a prey to the ignorance and the superstition of the age. The churches were shut up, the Gospel was not preached, the Holy Sabbath was neglected and profaned over the kingdom; the decency of morals gradually perished with religion. The way was thus paved for the deadly march of deism. Led on, at last, by Voltaire and his atheistic satellites, the frightful demon of infidelity filled France with its emissaries; these met with feeble opposition: truth had fallen in the streets, and her faithful watchmen were gone! Vice, and crime, and atheism, covered France. This conspiracy against God and man, burst forth in the old French revolution; and it buried the government, and religion, and morals, and the nation, in blood and havoc!

And as certainly as "a nation turns aside from the path, and causes the Holy One of Israel to cease from before them"; and as certainly as atheism, and licentious morals, and the contempt of the Sabbath and of the Gospel, pervade the land; so certainly will the same sanguinary scenes be acted over again, by its populace and its leading men; and the same desolating judgments sweep over the breadth and length of a nation!

This is according to the fundamental law of the Divine government, illustrated by the details of his holy providence, and recorded on the pages of history, both sacred and civil: NATIONAL SINS CALL FORTH NATIONAL JUDGMENTS; BUT NATIONS CAN BE PUNISHED FOR THEIR CRIMES, AS NATIONS, ONLY IN THIS WORLD. Hence follow those national calamities, and their final overthrow, sooner or later, if national penitence and reformation before the Most High, do not avert them!

We now arrive at the following conclusions, which we beg leave to submit to every Christian and patriot in our republic.

1. It is essential to the well-being and perpetuity of our free institutions, that knowledge be disseminated, and sound morals cherished assiduously, among those with whom the sovereign power is lodged; namely, the great body of the people.

2. Pure religion is the parent and nurse of all sound morals. The political virtues and the morality

of the men of the world are often but the mask of hypocrisy, and are, at best, of no endurance; they are easily overborne by temptation, for they have no life in them. They are a branch lopped off, and stuck in the ground: they may, for a season, exhibit some tokens of a feeble vegetation, but they want the root. Christian morality, on the contrary, is the green and fruitful branch: it grows out of the living tree, and bears rich and perennial fruits.

3. But true religion cannot exist, far less flourish, where the Gospel and its sacred institutions are not. No effect can exist without the means and the cause which produce it.

4. Hence, it is the part of genuine patriotism, as well as of Christianity, to spread the principles of our holy religion and sound morals over the country. An arbitrary princess was once constrained to declare, that she feared *John Knox's prayers more than ten thousand armed men opposed to her!* Truly, each Christian, who labors piously to spread the holy influence of religion and virtue around the circle in which he moves, is rearing the bulwark of his country's defense and glory, and has more of the pure patriotism of a republican than the most splendid orator, or the most gifted statesman, who contaminates, by his principles and example, the morals of the people, and offers mockery to religion.

5. Hence, it is one of the holiest and most solemn duties which a patriot owes his country, to

sustain the divine institutions of the Gospel, and to spread their moral influence over the community, by all proper and honorable means.

6. And hence, every Christian and patriot within our old states is bound, by all the obligations which they owe to their God and their country, zealously to employ all the means which heaven has put into their power, to procure a recognition and establishment of the Holy Sabbath in every new state, similar to what now exists in the old states; and to exert their personal influence, as Christian men, in propagating the Gospel of our Lord and Saviour Jesus Christ as extensively as possible among the citizens thereof.

7. And hence, also, it is a duty most solemnly binding on every republican, as a fearer of God and a lover of his country, when called, in his official character, to form the constitution and laws of a new state, carefully to give to the law protecting the sanctity of the Holy Sabbath, its just and prominent place; and also to employ all his personal weight and influence, as a Christian, in making and acquiring every facility to the spread of the blessed Gospel in the new settlements.

Here we rest our earnest appeal. These duties let every Christian and patriot perform, in his place, under the fear of Almighty God; and as he values the well-being and perpetuity of our free institutions. These duties let every one of us zealously perform, in the fear of the Judge of all the earth; and as we value the present happiness, and the everlasting salvation of millions of millions, yet unborn—the future citizens of these United States!

MAN'S QUESTIONS & GOD'S ANSWERS

Am I accountable to God?
Each of us will give an account of himself to God. ROMANS 14:12 (NIV).

Has God seen all my ways?
Everything is uncovered and laid bare before the eyes of him to whom we must give account. HEBREWS 4:13 (NIV).

Does he charge me with sin?
But the Scripture declares that the whole world is a prisoner of sin. GALATIANS 3:22 (NIV).
All have sinned and fall short of the glory of God. ROMANS 3:23 (NIV).

Will he punish sin?
The soul who sins is the one who will die. EZEKIEL 18:4 (NIV).
For the wages of sin is death, but the gift of God is eternal life in Christ Jesus our Lord. ROMANS 6:23 (NIV).

Must I perish?
He is patient with you, not wanting anyone to perish, but everyone to come to repentance. 2 PETER 3:9 (NIV).

How can I escape?
Believe in the Lord Jesus, and you will be saved. ACTS 16:31 (NIV).

Is he able to save me?
Therefore he is able to save completely those who come to God through him. HEBREWS 7:25 (NIV).

Is he willing?
Christ Jesus came into the world to save sinners. 1 TIMOTHY 1:15 (NIV).

Am I saved on believing?
Whoever believes in the Son has eternal life, but whoever rejects the Son will not see life, for God's wrath remains on him. JOHN 3:36 (NIV).

Can I be saved now?
Now is the time of God's favor, now is the day of salvation. 2 CORINTHIANS 6:2 (NIV).

As I am?
Whoever comes to me I will never drive away. JOHN 6:37 (NIV).

Shall I not fall away?
Him who is able to keep you from falling. JUDE 1:24 (NIV).

If saved, how should I live?
Those who live should no longer live for themselves but for him who died for them and was raised again. 2 CORINTHIANS 5:15 (NIV).

What about death and eternity?
I am going there to prepare a place for you. I will come back and take you to be with me that you also may be where I am. JOHN 14:2-3 (NIV).